Honoring Grief

Honoring Grief

Poems by

Susan A. Wright

© 2025 Susan A. Wright. All rights reserved.
This material may not be reproduced in any form, published,
reprinted, recorded, performed, broadcast,
rewritten or redistributed without
the explicit permission of Susan A. Wright.
All such actions are strictly prohibited by law.

Cover design by Shay Culligan
Cover image by Tianhao Wang

ISBN: 978-1-63980-763-5

Kelsay Books
502 South 1040 East, A-119
American Fork, Utah 84003
Kelsaybooks.com

I dedicate this volume to
Dr. William Neal, Dr. Robert Doty, and Amanda Melheim
for their inspiration and assistance.

These poems honor the deaths of
Ralph Wright, Dr. William Neal, and Dr. Beth Kemper,
among others.

Acknowledgments

Thank you to the following publications, in which versions of these poems previously appeared:

Connections: "Paint a Picture"
The Russell Creek Review: "From the Grave," "Shrine," "There Will Not Be Time," "Elegy for Numbness"

Contents

Part I. *Honoring Grief*

Nov. 3rd	13
From the Grave	14
The Clock	15
A Planet Created in Your Name (Shrine I)	16
A Gray Moth of Grief (Shrine II)	19
I Push Aside All Heaven (Shrine III)	22
Stone and Vines: The Beloved's View (Shrine IV)	26
It Is Satisfactory	31
A Boy's Soul Melts	33
Not the Worst	34
Fires and Falling Trees	36
Denial and a Donut for Supper	38
Elegy for Numbness	39
There Will Not Be Time	40
Memorial for Clay Hill Memorial Forest	42

Part II. *Reflections*

The Transformation of Imagination	47
Mr. Nice Guy	48
Seasons	51
Deaf Gain	52
American Sign Language	54
The Shadow of Stars	55
Silver Water	56
Paint a Picture	58
I Will Find the Ladder Myself	59
Bridge	61
Love Reveals Itself As . . .	63
Lockdown, April 2020	64

Part I.

Honoring Grief

Nov. 3rd

When I enter the hospital room,
you are dead—
I see it in the way
you lie collapsed on the bed.
You gasp—
a final breath, a reflex.
I touch your cheek and say, "I love you."
The nurse whispers,
"Oh, honey, it's so much easier this way."
Your pain and indignity cease.
I kiss your cooling forehead.
I am never the same.

From the Grave

in memory of Dr. William Neal

In my dream, you stand by the window
in the foyer of Carter Hall.
I top the stairs, and shocked
to find you alive,
I run down to greet you.
Dirt streaks your leather jacket.
You are the same height as my father,
who died twelve years earlier
to the day.
The call came the same hour.

But, abruptly, you live again,
laughing, smiling, speaking,
"It was simply a mistake.
I've climbed from my grave.
I'm covered in dirt,
but I hardly care."

A student sees you from the hallway,
shouts your name, and hugs you.
I stare through the window as
people pass on the sidewalk,
oblivious to the relief of our reunion.

Then I awaken.
There is no you,
no trail of dirt.
Only honoring grief.

The Clock

Your chest no longer rises with breath.
Time ticks like
a bomb in my heart, counting
down the days, hours, minutes,
until someone else I love
rests in a shiny steel casket.

A dozen deaths, funerals, dirges later
I comprehend my breath
must also cease,
my chest falling still.
The dim stars, the looming moon,
our spiral galaxy,
the vast, sparkling expanse of our
asymmetrical universe
will all pass away.
I wait with all creation,
the clock hands ticking,
to transform into star dust.

A Planet Created in Your Name
(Shrine I)

I'll build an altar to act
as your memorial:
Black stone inset with stars
to glitter on clear nights.
Space was your obsession;
I'll find you nowhere else
except the heavens,
my explorer, my scientist, my love.

I'll pray your soul
not out of purgatory
but to another planet.
Let heaven be a life elsewhere,
where children's games are
secret joyous hunts.
You won't admit your delight,
but you'll chase me
up streets of crimson dust.
You'll hide in jungle-gardens
where the roses are jasmine-scented,
lavender buds shaped
like cupped human hands.
You'll raise an eyebrow, suppress a smile.

The lights in space are God winking;
I'll pick the brightest blue glimmer
to be your sun.
I'll join you after machines
no longer prolong my death.
Let heaven be a life elsewhere,
where clean desert floors
replace grassy lawns
and with the dawn rises
a sister planet like Saturn.

We'll see rings every morning when we wake.
We'll climb in shuttles to gas giants
or stand on mountain ridges at sunset
to watch crimson rays
wash the sands bloody.
Your eyes will shine at such beauty,
but your appreciation will pass unspoken.

We'll be reborn with wings or
black and lithe like panthers.
When we galaxy hop in spaceships,
we'll stop to gaze at Earth and laugh.

You made a papier-mâché planet
for third grade science.
You kept it because other planets
and spiral galaxies entranced you.
If I sacrifice the lumpy blue ball on the altar,
will God create a planet in your name?

I'll pray your soul to another planet.
You'll walk on rose-colored
stone paths to the haunting calls
of lizard-birds. Once I die
I'll stand at your side and tell you
you're Kipling's Thousandth Man.
Finally, you'll laugh,
and it'll explode the galaxy.

As you died you grasped my hand
the first and last time.
You faded like a shadow at sunset.
I pretended not to cry,
but you saw and touched my tears
as though you'd never seen such drops before.

You called me beloved.
I would have killed the universe for you.
I'll build you an altar and paint the galaxy on its top.
I'll mark the brightest star as yours—
a shrine.

A Gray Moth of Grief
(Shrine II)

The hardest part is walking away
from your shiny steel coffin,
your waxy face against a satin backdrop.
My hand reaches inside
and touches your arm one last time.
A car ride, a bus trip, a spaceship . . .
how I leave the funeral could be anything.

The trip home after you die
is a metallic-tasting nightmare
scorching my tongue
and back-drafting into my nose.
My eyes sting.
Silence booms like bell-tolls;
I ride without sight or sound.
Time creeps like geological periods as I travel.
A gray moth of grief bats in my head,
blindly bumps my inner skull;
galaxies explode in white bursts, return to protomatter.
Am I yin without yang or yang without yin?
The loss of you is an increase of entropy,
the death of the universe.

You once said you'd fall off
the mythic flat edge of the universe
for me—
a most solemn vow.

I loved your solemnity, your quiet darkness.
Now I stand at the edge of the universe
and peer at dimming red galaxies,
blue superclusters,
finger-shaped rainbow nebulas.
Beside them, Earth is a dust mote.
I lean, I teeter, and, dizzy, I fall.
In the cold, hard vacuum,
my capillaries rupture.

The tears on my face might be blood.
Or is it that the blood might be tears?

I sit in your room for hours,
burn your sandalwood incense,
stare at the painting of God
casting Adam and Eve from Eden,
and know I can never
summon the right words,
never express our bond.
I can sing or cry or talk or wail
and never empty myself of grief.

At night, I gaze at the ever-present stars
but see the two teardrops that escaped
the corners of your eyes at death.
The image of your set face,
both like you and not,
haunts my closed eyelids.

I hate the whole world.

Only the vastness of the universe eases my pain.
Stars are so numerous that
100,000 galaxies could be a grain of sand
held at arm's length.
Yes, my friend, I take comfort in the thought
the universe will end.
I take comfort in the entropy
that is death.

I Push Aside All Heaven
(Shrine III)

On the third day, the desert I dream of
becomes reality—
Baking heat, hard-packed, crimson sand,
the face of the sister planet in the night sky:
A face scarred with the angry gashes of canyons.
Volcanic blemishes bleed fiery oranges.
I stand in awe at the terrifying orb
that fills half the night sky;
I've found your new home.
At this journey's end, I will find you.

I'll push aside all heaven,
claw away all the earth to find you.

The desert stretches—a giant
elongating his back after sleep—
in endless tans and crimsons.
Each tiny grain of sand glitters
in the light of the sister planet,
like the star-filled sky has fallen to earth
for me to tread in my quest.
In the distance, the giant's backbone—
a sharp, black mountain range—rises.
I walk toward the tallest vertebrae-peak.
The impact of the steps rings in my knees,
and my feet go numb.

A soul-deep, primal voice within
urges me forward.
If I complete the pilgrimage,
you will return to me.
Toward dawn, dust builds in a black wall,
arching behind me.

A tsunami of sand stabs toward heaven,
rushes across the endless expanse,
howls, wails, vomits its bowels through its throat,
and bellows that it will eat my soul,
swallow my essence whole like a snake.

The gales drive sand into my skin
like metallic splinters.
I forgot how to cry when you died,
and I only dully register pain now.
I crouch in the sand like an animal
and close my eyes against the black tornado
that blasts off my flesh.
If it is a skeleton that stumbles
to the foot of your mountain, your soul's retreat,
would you still recognize me?
My spirit struggles, creates a ball in the storm's throat;
it digests me intact like any common rodent.

When I emerge at last into calm daylight,
with bleeding skin and limp rags,
I see vast white sands and a black mountain peak,
upright and royal:
The queen mystery of the desert.
Silent.
Still.
An ancient world, this desert and its mountain,
with their buried knowledge
and aloof distance.
But I would spill the blood from my own heart
to shatter that curtain of arrogant privacy,
would surrender my innermost mind
to intimate revelation—
pry it open to reveal tender, painful vulnerabilities—
if it would return you to me.

On the baking breeze I hear your dry chuckle.
From the shimmering sand before me, water mirages
fade into your shape, solid and real.
Your white robe flaps and rustles in the wind.
Strands of your black hair
try to fly away as the deep, red sun
evokes a shine at your crown.
Wrinkles crease your wise face,
now free of suffering,
and your dark eyes reflect the sunlight.
You smile, your teeth white.

"Do you see now?" you ask in a soft, deep voice.
"You are not here for my return, but your own."

Your gentle laughter tickles my ears.
My eyes look past you to the white sands
that give way to carved stone stairs,
thousands of steps up the serene mountain.
A stillness settles the air.

You extend the hand I grasped but once in life.
I take it, almost like a child,
and am comforted by its warm skin.
Such a luxury to have you present
to lead me anywhere.
"Welcome home," you say.
You squeeze my hand,
and we walk up the stairs
together.

Stone and Vines: The Beloved's View (Shrine IV)

In the garden, spindly black vines bind
the Madonna statue in ropes of leaves.
The statue reaches out her stone arms to me,
a gesture I can never copy.
My hand extends to touch you, my beloved,
but you're only a carving in my mind.
Black vines pull my arms to my sides
to stop my forbidden touch.
The wind through the trees rustles leaves like laughter,
laughter at my thoughts.
Best my thoughts remain unspoken.

I kneel at the feet of a stone Madonna,
a cement Mother of God.
I worship the mold covering her toes
or pray to Father God,
but for all my worship and prayers,
I will forever be
Untouchable.
I may whisper to stone ears of my need to love,
be loved. Touched.
That I need the sadness, the sweetness of love
and all the pain it brings.
But I'll sit and watch black vines grow another inch
for all the peace it will bring.

It's my skin.

In the garden I may be free,
but I must return to the world in the morning
and feel the pain of lack, the pain of longing,
a tearing with every step I take through dull cement halls.

With every ring of every step on cold tile floors,
my heart reaches out,
but I swallow that cry just behind each breath.
I allow black vines to twist tighter around my chest.

My friend, you turn to me, human perfection,
with all your beauty, assertiveness,
inner torment, and guilt.
No one as perfect as you could need me,
much less love me
as a friend, a confidant, a lover.
But you smile at me—
that special smile, the one you reserve for me.
Can I really be that beloved?
Black vines tighten briefly, but the leaves wilt.
(Does the carving in my mind reach out farther?
Can stone statues move?)
You've said to me, "I need you."
Or I've heard you say, "I need him."
And after a time, I realize it's not just my skills.
It's me: my mind, my thoughts, my soul.

But there's the problem of my heritage.

If I press my forehead to the coolness
of the Madonna statue's feet
and bathe her with secret tears,
if I scrape some holy mold
underneath a fingernail in faith,
will my heart be healed?
Could you reach across the cultural
and social expanse of night and
touch me?
For you strive to follow my rule:
Don't touch.

My father didn't.
My mother was restrained.
The school children were statues
with their eyes ever averted.
Not a social politeness,
an aversion to touching
my skin.
I, a modern-day leper,
thrown from house, from town—
seen but untouchable.

How I love those moments you forget yourself
and clap a hand on my shoulder.
No revulsion.
All the vines wilt.
The statue inside crumbles with movement,
if only for a moment.

I imagine my garden Madonna smile,
and I think you'll never know
how I wish to touch in return—
the nearly physical bleeding from the need
to tell you how special you are to me.
How you don't see my skin, my eyes, my hair,
all those markers of difference.
How they don't mean a damn thing to you,
because when you talk about the person inside
you're not waxing pious.

The day you touch my cheek, I nearly die.
I spend five hours in my garden meditating,
trying not to react, to stop the urge
to smile, to laugh, to cry.

I tell stone Madonna all about you,
confess you,
even grab her lifeless hand
and kiss her black vines.
I ask her why God
brought me into life this way.
But the wind blows and the leaves laugh
and I remember
why I don't speak my heart.

Then I curse my father
for denying me my mother
and making sure I understand
the depth of the shame it is
to be me.

Black vines bloom again.

Yet you clap my shoulders with your hands
in the closest to a hug I may come,
and the blooms wilt again.
If only, if only the pleasure of it
doesn't reach my face.
If I can exit the room with dignity
and pretend the touch doesn't matter.
But I know you see the shine
that lights my dark eyes.
I think when I die, I shall die for you.
I think you will search the universe for me.
I think you will follow me.
If only once I could return the words
and tell you how much I care for you.
But my lips become like Madonna's stone.

What will it say, what will it say,
my soul, when it is ripped apart?
I love you, a whisper in my heart.

It Is Satisfactory

How regal a father you seem:
broad shoulders, erect spine,
a snow-dust of white in your dark hair,
bushy eyebrows over narrowed brown eyes,
valleys of facial lines to indicate levels of displeasure.
I look up to you.

Golden sunlight on late summer days
lengthens your shadow as you stroll
stone garden paths to where I sulk.
Other children had taunted me with names;
bloody knuckles and a split lip
show my answer. I look into your eyes
for understanding, for grace.
But your sharp eyes glitter,
your voice cracking like a whip:
"Son, violence is not the way!"

I strive to stoke your pride,
fan its flames to burn,
by making the highest grades,
winning awards,
taking first place.
Each evening as you recline in your chair,
I approach and kneel, offering
my day's academic accomplishment
on the altar of your parental demands.
Your response:
"It is satisfactory."

Satisfactory.

Abandoning your altar,
I enlist in the military
and travel the world,
lands green, oceans blue,
far away from you.
Our silence spans fifteen years.
An empty chair sits for you at my wedding.

When you die, I'm fighting overseas
in a war for peace.
Peace is for the dead.
I come home to your grave,
where your pride has sealed
behind your bloodless lips
anger about my childhood bullies
and joy about my accomplishments.
Your love remains forever unspoken.
Father, I cannot say, "Satisfactory."

A Boy's Soul Melts

A shot cracks the stillness.
His hand and arm jerk backward,
his wrist stings, his shoulder burns.
His sister screams.

> The musty scent of old paperbacks
> and dry-rotting leather bindings
> cling to her nostrils. The world
> fragments into a flash
> of sunlight from the window. Panic
> on her brother's face. The thud
> of a pistol hitting the wooden desk,
> the carpeted floor. The salty tang of blood
> on her tongue. The brilliant glare
> of heaven's window. The acidic
> smell as a boy's soul melts.

A circular spray of blood on the wall
marks how the bullet pierced his sister's chest.
A game of soldiers, a game of cops and robbers,
drug addicts and dealers, gone wrong—
his voice cracks, his soul chokes,
he smashes fists against his eyes.
A real gun shoots a real bullet.

Not the Worst

After your funeral,
fascination with death
sucks me in like Charybdis.
While vacuuming, I see the news:
man in pond of blood,
child with bullet hole in back.
Pictures flash across the TV screen;
a deep female voice intones,
"courthouse massacre"
and "school shooting."
The pictures magnetize me,
but the reality of death slips away
like the ghost of a soul-eater
during the new moon.

I turn my car onto a side street,
mind on a mundane grocery trip,
but my gaze shifts sideways to the cemetery.
Neat gray rows of granite
crosses, Madonnas, hearts, plaques.
A family buried a seven-year-old girl yesterday—
death by accidental shooting.
Did they have one of those little coffins?
A stray wish to see it
flits through my mind:
a peaceful child's face before me,
a small head on a miniature pillow.
I'd compare it to those I've seen.

Then, faced with the little girl's loss,
I tell myself my grief is not
the worst.

I don't heal.

Fires and Falling Trees

in memory of Ralph Wright

Your death lives in my nightmares.
In my dreamscape, I stroll across
the crunchy, brown grass
of my childhood front yard.
Dusk settles like blood rimming blue eyes.
You sit under the Bradford pear tree,
glasses perched on the end of your nose,
reading the news
and smoking a King Edward cigar.
I kneel to speak with you,
only to watch the cigar fall
from your lips in dream-style slow motion.
The tree bursts into orange horns of flame.

I scream for you to move, to run,
but a crack like a snapping neck announces
the tree as it falls
and crushes you underneath.
The fire spreads from tree to house then house to house.
I scream, cheeks streaked with sooty tears,
as flames devour you
and my childhood home burns.
The heat scorches my skin.

The fire surrounds me.
Fire trucks blare onto the scene,
but the water is an impotent,
bent slave
propelled in vain
from rubber snakes.

A helicopter arrives to lift me to safety.
I hold onto the landing bar—
no time, space, or care
to stow me safely inside.

We rise above, but my hand is slipping.

The next morning, I stroll
through the gray snow-dusting of ash,
all that remains of our house.
The stench of smoke sears my nose.
It is no longer a home.
We lost you.

Last night I dreamt of fires and falling trees.

Denial and a Donut for Supper

White tile outside the OR,
a cool breeze from swinging doors,
fluorescent lights humming, pink walls,
male voices droning on TV,
the stench of stale coffee.

"They're removing the tumor now."
"How is he?"
"Stable."

Hours of phone calls, hushed voices,
chewed nails, prayers and pleas,
and nurses with squeaky shoes.
"In recovery for 45 minutes."

More like 90.
Beeps and yells interrupt calm doctor voices.
I pass the time with
denial and a donut for supper.
Finally, I visit my snoring father,
the nightmare paused for now.

Elegy for Numbness

They'll bury another child today,
the earth so baked and dry they'll strain to dig a grave;
the dirt will crumble as they fill the hole.
Scorched summer grass won't grow there,
and the mother won't allow brown leaves to rot there.
Snow will come, and she will say, "Poetic."
Her soul freezes and lodges itself in her throat.
If only she could squeeze a scream past the lump.

I gaze at the neighboring cemetery from my porch.
Frost bites my nose, but sweat lines discolor my shirt.
I don't just watch the black hearses, I follow them:
my grandparents, parents, and friends.
Grief takes out my hair in clumps
until Novocain fills my soul. Soon
they'll bury another son or daughter, mother or father,
pet dog, severed hand, marriage, religious faith.
Flush a gold fish down the toilet bowl.

If I'm allowed to bury anything,
let it be my numbness.

Don't leave a marker.

There Will Not Be Time

in memory of Dr. Beth Kemper

The day you died,
I learned to snap bones in karate class.
After an hour's drive home,
I found the red blinking of the answering machine.
Repeated calls announce despair,
and this one in a wavering voice said, "Beth has died."
That ten seconds between words and comprehension
is the eternity between peace and anguish.

On days when an imagination is a curse,
I see you trapped behind the car wheel—
I see your eyes unseeing,
metal and glass shattered on the pavement,
and I finally understand the cliché of
"There are no guarantees."

How can I eulogize?
What can I say of laughs like fluttering wings,
of late-night sanity calls,
of inside jokes about Prufrock?
"There will be time, there will be time."
But there will not.

At the funeral, I sit with a pile of soggy Kleenex,
under the weight of choked eulogies,
watching weeping parents.
I'm angry at the boy
who dares to laugh in the hallway.

I fail at goodbyes.
When life is ripped away,
and my last memory is a white casket,
I achieve no closure.

Memorial for Clay Hill Memorial Forest

December 2021,
I stand in a gravel parking lot,
stare at tree trunks twisted,
snapped,
branches stripped bare,
the weekly, sometimes daily,
refuge of my soul flattened
by a tornado.

The man beside me holds out
a small screen,
shows me footage from his drone:
tree toothpicks
lined up like pencils
in a child's school box
and a random shed blasted
by a wind bomb,
wood and metal spewed over
frozen earth.

Tree trunks lie dead among
brethren who stand strong,
ancient roots upturned
and bared to the pale sky.
The sun shines as if
no storm had torn through.
The cold bites my nose
as I understand every trail I walked
lies buried, erased,
my favorite hill flat and naked,
my natural sanctuary remote, hidden.

The sun sets across splintered wood
as I mourn my friend,
my companion for silent walks
and private contemplations.
While the forest will regrow,
I'll pass away before it stands tall again.

Just like life:
Something or someone
beloved
killed in an instant.

Part II.

Reflections

The Transformation of Imagination

Childhood:
castles are made of books
for plastic ponies to inhabit.
Washing machines are mountains,
shoeboxes ships,
and rulers walking planks.
Couches are stages,
tennis rackets guitars,
beds trampolines.
Barbie walks carpeted streets,
swims in a slimy plastic pool,
and talks with Skipper about my dream life.

Adolescence:
From toys to boys,
jewelry, makeup, curling irons—
Barbie lies on the brown carpet,
and no play voices grace my lips.
Silenced.

During English class I pick up a pen,
find my voice again.
My characters stroll through my school
in an alternate universe,
one suave but sweet,
the other confident and charismatic.
My orange locker and green desk
become words on a page, a stage.

Mr. Nice Guy

Books, books, books,
cream-colored pages
and black ink discuss
covert narcissists, covert abusers,
the insidious crawl of verbal violence.
"If he really knew how much he hurt me,
he wouldn't say it."
Lies, lies, lies.

On a red, leather couch
I sit and wait for the lawyer.
Papers, papers, papers
rush in and save me.
26 years of my adult life
circling around the toilet bowl
as I finally flush
over two decades of
insincere compliments,
feigned empathy
twisted into manipulation,
and red-faced fits of "jealousy."

Because knowledge brings wisdom,
I hope.
Little black letters on a cream-colored page
flipped the light switch in my brain,
flooding the gray matter with white light:
Jealousy is not jealousy.
Possessiveness wearing a red jealousy cape
is a man's way to control
his partner.

As a teenager, I sat in his car
thinking, "He said his ex hurt him
because she cheated on him.
He's so insecure and vulnerable now,
he gets jealous of every man I meet—"
Like my English professor,
my boss,
and the man at the cash register.
"But I should be a good little
Christian girl
and forgive him."
So he can do it again.

Until those little black letters
in those books penned by experts
rammed the truth
through my squishy gray matter
like a steel rod covered in ice:
It's never jealousy.
And he chased away my friends,
male and female,
young and old,
close and casual
until it was a ghost town of two.
Tumbleweeds rolled in the wind
through a dusty street,
and still his red-faced "jealousy" raged
that I was never happy enough to see him,

never smiled brightly enough
when he came through the door,
and why was I losing weight
except to get a new boyfriend?

Control is never enough control
until I am fixed and gray,
unbreathing in my steel coffin,
the iron bands of his grip
having crushed my lungs
privately, privately, privately.

Because in public he's
Mr. Nice Guy.

Seasons

Fall: fog wraps filmy white arms
around houses like a cat
winds around its owner's legs.

Winter: snow covers the yard in drifts
that swell into white hills
which sparkle in the sun.

Spring: rain splashes into puddles,
creating miniature fountains
of intricate, circular design.

Summer: sunshine glows,
warms bare arms and legs.
Flies buzz and bounce against windows,
and the world lives again.

Deaf Gain

The day I accept my hearing loss,
I notice my peripheral vision can show me
my white front door on the left
and my white stove on the right
without my moving my head.

No, I can't read lips.
But I appreciate every scrap of voice,
every sharp or flat note,
every dog barking,
with what hearing remains.

"It's not hearing loss.
It's deaf gain."

As my toes slip into the warm water
of the d/Deaf world,
I read the closed captioning as
people sign their words.
Deaf Gain is
to sleep in silence;
it's deliverance from
TVs that blare,
phones that beep,
cars that honk,
neighbors that yell.

People say, "I would kill myself
if I couldn't hear music."
But I will play piano
even if my remaining hearing slips away.

Like Beethoven, I will rest my face on the wood
and feel the notes vibrate
in my chest, my heart,
my spirit,
and I will not grieve the "loss."

American Sign Language

My fingers talk,
a c for *C,*
and a d for *D.*
My arms fold, rock,
signing "baby."
"I" is a finger point
to my chest,
and I think,
"Learning a second language
was supposed to be difficult.
Why didn't I do this
sooner?"
I tap my thumb to my forehead,
fingers splayed,
for "father,"
my thumb to my chin
for "mother,"
and with every gesture, every
Sign
walk into the world
of the d/Deaf
with pride.

The Shadow of Stars

I live in the shadow of stars,
dwell in the corners of dreams,
but within my hidden heart I see
fragments of those who walk beside me:
a wisp of auburn hair, a flapping blue cloak—
a yellow butterfly, a purple feather,
images like a stained glass window.

As I walk from desert to forest,
I pass plucked fairy wings,
gilded carriages, dragons' bones,
starved children, and proud unicorns
without a spark of curiosity
to warm the fog in my chest.

But what prize is it for me
to dwell at the edges of nightmares?
What gift is it to move into the starlight?
To hear an elf's laugh, see a boy's smile?
To feel the wind upon my face
or to smell thick forest pine?
To touch a lover's smooth skin?

Can starlight make those fragments bloom?

Silver Water

Through lacy curtains
I watch the rain hang
like drapes upon the world.
A dank smell invades the house;
a ticking clock marks the time loss.
But I flee outside to feel
warm droplets on my face.

In the driveway I kneel,
stretching my fingers toward silver water
pooling in the dipping pavement.
The gray sky ripples
in the rainwater mirror.
As I lean closer, the silver
puddle mirrors me:
dark hair bleeding silver with time.
Sheets of rain threaten to pour
melancholy into my silver soul.

I stand, retrace my steps
on the wet pavement,
and inhale the sweet spring scent
of flowers and rain—
the natural world.
A gentle mist caresses my skin,
reminding me that both spring and fall
are indelible phases of life.

Brilliant green leaves and pink blossoms
glow against the gray sky,
illuminated by the contrast.
Facing the gray, I open my arms to
silver rain, silver hair, silver life.
Beyond the rain, beyond the gray,
I stretch my hand into eternity.

Paint a Picture

A dictionary palette,
notebook paper on the easel:

The southward wind warms my face;
the cloudless sunset stretches above me
like paint strokes of orange, gold, and rose.

Tucked deep in the countryside,
a sparkling, cold creek tickles my feet.
The spring babbles secrets to me.

The raw earth awes me with mountain peaks;
I lope through emerald-carpeted fields,
soft grass alive under my bare feet.

Once inside, I paint my picture with words;
I etch the countryside on my soul.

I Will Find the Ladder Myself

with a bow to Wilfred Owen

I stumble through the gray,
the world a flat, toneless
void.
Arms heavy, legs heavy, soul heavy—
Can I not just lie in bed
a few minutes-hours-days longer?
Fused to the pillow, lovers with the blanket,
blackout curtains drawn. Hidden.
Thoughts firing like dogfighters
crash me into the earth. I explode.

Depression circles into itself,
an ouroboros of gray granite.

I drag through my days, hauling
my carcass behind me.
Death circles over each thought.
I find a perfect numb repetition:
Leave, return, bed.
Leave, return, bed.
Doctors, preachers, friends circle me,
cawing like crows:
"Do you have no faith in God?"
"Pray harder."
"Read psalms."
"Just be more thankful."
"Why can't you pull yourself together?"
"Snap out of it."
"Stiff upper lip."
"Man-up."
"Grab those bootstraps and haul."

Depression is an internal five-nine,
a mud-filled trench in World War I.
Crimson froth wets my lips,
mustard gas burns my lungs.
Under a sea of darkness, I plunge at you,
gutter, groan.
With bloody bandages stained dark,
I hit the ground as each shell screams;
fears explode through my chest like shrapnel.
If you had seen this war as I have,
you would not breed platitudes
of toxic positivity.
King David's songs will not save me.
And if prayer alone could save me,
I would have emerged brighter
than a flare in the dark night of Germany.

When I climb out of the trenches,
I will find the ladder myself.

Bridge

I lie in the soft grass beside the creek.
The clear water rushes
over smooth, brown stones,
only to slow at the bend,
where a miniature delta
grows out of rich, black silt.
How long has the creek labored
in its thoughtless, impulsive way
to build this delta
and catch a stick to create
a natural dam, a bridge for ants
to carry supper home?

I meditate upon the ants
as I await word of my future.
Opposite me stretch woods
with trails that, like my future, diverge,
leading a traveler to vastly different lives.
But to reach the trails I need a bridge—
one to carry me from youth to old age.

As I lie on the bank, a storm
like an ocean falls
in sheets from the sky.
Black clouds roil,
lightning flashes in fury,
the creek swells and sweeps away
the fragile silt delta.
Clumps of earth drown in the torrent;
the dam dissolves, wrecking
the bridge for hardworking ants.

How many bridges wash away?
How many trails vanish in the downpour?

I stand, my feet sinking in the mud,
and peer into the shadowy woods.
I pray, "Don't make me walk on water."
When the rain clears, can I build
a bridge to carry me?
I will my path to appear.

Love Reveals Itself As . . .

Typed words on a smart phone:
Absentee, distracted, distant, anxious, and stressed;

Still mentally at work in a gray cubicle:
Cerebral, untouchable, rule-bound, and oppressive;

Warming a wooden church pew:
Rigid, judgmental, and harshly punishing the disobedient;

Red-faced screams:
Possessive, insecure, pushy, controlling, and hateful;

Circles with a narcissist's vulture-like wings:
Drain, consume, nitpick, rinse, and repeat;

A pillow pressed to my face at midnight:
Rejected perseverance, false reassurance, and finally suffocation.

Lockdown, April 2020

Silence, stillness, peace.
I mute my laptop,
close the lid on the news,
walk to the window.
No cars drive past.
Anxiety hums along my nerves—
"Will my loved ones die?"—
but fades at the sight of pink buds,
tiny green leaves.
The world returns to life
amidst an ocean's swell of death.

In the forest, my boots snap twigs,
maple leaves unfurl,
oak leaves sprout,
and mockingbirds sing,
contrasting with my thoughts:
"Will I lose my remaining family,
small as it is,
before the fall?
Before Christmas?"
But no cars drive past;
the world remains hushed.
Silence, stillness, peace.

About the Author

Writing poetry has been part of Dr. Susan Wright's life since she was fourteen, and she was published in *Creative Kids* magazine during high school. Her publishing history includes poems in anthologies and journals such as *Low Explosions: Writings on the Body, Secrets of the Soul, The Russell Creek Review, Crossroads, Connections,* and *The Campbellsville Review.*

Dr. Wright earned her MA in English with an emphasis in Creative Writing, and her creative thesis was directed by Sena Jeter Naslund. She earned her PhD in Composition from the University of Louisville.

Currently, Dr. Wright teaches English at a small private university and lives in Kentucky with her cat.

Visit her at:
drsusanawright.wixsite.com/poet

www.ingramcontent.com/pod-product-compliance
Lightning Source LLC
Chambersburg PA
CBHW030914170426
43193CB00009BA/844